Birds A to Z

by Terri DeGezelle

Consultant:
Ilze Balodis,
Institute for Field Ornithology,
University of Maine at Machias

W9-AOC-698

Books

Capstone Curriculum Publishing
Mankato, Minnesota

Aa

The albatross is the largest seabird. Seabirds live by the ocean. The albatross can sleep while it flies.

Albatross

Aa Bb Cc Dd Ee Ff Gg Hh Ii Jj Kk Ll Mm Nn Oo Pp Qq Rr Ss Tt Uu Vv Ww Xx Yy Zz

Bb

Bobolink

Bobolinks build their nests by digging into the dirt in an area with tall grasses. The female bobolink will run through the grass to get away from the nest before she takes flight. This way, she hides the location of her eggs or nestlings.

Cc

Chickadee

Chickadees will hang upside down from branches and bird feeders as they eat. If you come up to a mother chickadee and her babies, the mother will hiss at you like a snake.

Doves are the smallest and fastest members of the pigeon family. They can fly 55 miles an hour. Doves are not good nest builders. Their nests often fall apart on stormy days.

Dd

Dove

Ee

Bald eagles are large birds. They can have a wingspan of eight feet and weigh 15 pounds. Eagle nests are about four feet across and three feet deep.

Eagle

Aa Bb Cc Dd **Ee** Ff Gg Hh Ii Jj Kk Ll Mm Nn Oo Pp Qq Rr Ss Tt Uu Vv Ww Xx Yy Zz

Ff

Flamingo

Flamingos are swamp birds. They build their nests out of mud. Flamingos scoop up big mouthfuls of muddy water to find their food.

Gg

Goldfinch

The mother goldfinch stays in the nest with her babies. The father brings home food for all of them. The mother eats the food, then throws it up and feeds it to the babies.

The hummingbird can fly backwards, forwards, straight up and down, and sideways. Hummingbirds can even hover in front of a flower to get a drink of nectar.

Hh

Hummingbird

Ii

The ibis lays two or three eggs in a season. The eggs hatch about 21 days after they are laid. The nestlings are born with their eyes closed. They sleep for the first week of life.

Ibis

Jj

Jay

Jays eat bugs, fruits, acorns, and the eggs and young of other birds. They are loud and noisy birds. To chase their enemies away, jays will fly directly at them and make loud noises.

Kk

The killdeer nests on the open ground. The nest is a hole in the dirt lined with pebbles and grass. The killdeer will limp as if it has a broken wing to lead enemies away from its nest and babies.

Killdeer

Aa Bb Cc Dd Ee Ff Gg Hh Ii Jj **Kk** Ll Mm Nn Oo Pp Qq Rr Ss Tt Uu Vv Ww Xx Yy Zz

Ll

Loon

Loons dive deep into lake water to fish for food. They can dive as deep as 30 feet and can stay under water for a full minute. Loons catch the fish with their bills.

Mm

Mockingbird

The mockingbird copies the songs of other birds. It can also croak like frogs, bark like dogs, and even scream like a siren. The mockingbird sings its own song too. The mockingbird's song is hard to copy.

Nightingales are members of the thrush family. The name nightingale means "night song." The name was given to them because they sing such a beautiful song.

Nn

Nightingale

Oo

Ostrich

The ostrich is the largest bird. It lays the largest egg of any bird. The egg weighs about three pounds. An adult ostrich can be bigger than an adult human. They grow to nine feet tall and weigh up to 330 pounds.

Puffins are seabirds. Puffins dive deep into the ocean to fish for food. They can hold their breath for as long as a minute. Puffins flap their wings and run across the water's surface when they want to fly.

Pp

Puffin

Qq

Quails live in groups called coveys. Members of a covey watch for enemies and find food together. As a part of a covey, it is easier to survive the winter.

Quail

Rr

Roadrunner

Roadrunners live in flat desert areas. They run fast in flat places. Roadrunners use their long, fast legs to chase prey. They eat bugs, snakes, and lizards.

Ss

Swan

The trumpeter swan is the largest kind of waterfowl. It can weigh 30 pounds and measure six feet from bill to tail. Its wingspan can be as wide as eight feet. To fly, it needs up to 20 feet of water to take off.

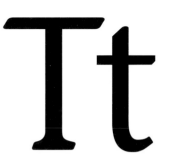

Wild turkeys are powerful flyers. They sleep in trees at night, but nest on the ground. Turkeys make a gobble-gobble sound.

Turkey

Uu

Upland sandpipers scratch their nests into the dirt. They lay leaves and grass in the bottom of the nest to make it softer. They hang prairie grass over the nest to hide it from enemies.

Upland Sandpiper

Aa Bb Cc Dd Ee Ff Gg Hh Ii Jj Kk Ll Mm Nn Oo Pp Qq Rr Ss Tt **Uu** Vv Ww Xx Yy Zz

Vv

Vulture

Vultures are birds that mainly eat carrion. Carrion is anything that is dead. When vultures find something to eat, they fly in circles above the dead animal, so other vultures can find it too.

Ww

Woodpecker

The woodpecker uses its pointed beak to drill or peck holes in wood. The woodpecker then reaches into the holes with its long, sticky tongue and pulls out bugs.

Xanthocephalus xanthocephalus is the name that ornithologists, people who study birds, give to the yellow-headed blackbird. The name gives information about where the bird lives, what it eats, or what birds belong to the same family.

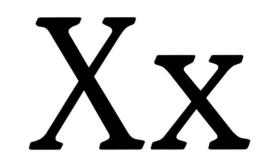

Xanthocephalus Xanthocephalus

Yy

Yellow-billed Oxpecker

The yellow-billed oxpecker rides on big animals, like giraffes, zebras, and oxen. It eats the ticks and other bugs that bother the animal. When an enemy is near, the yellow-billed oxpecker will hide behind the animal's ear or nose.

Aa Bb Cc Dd Ee Ff Gg Hh Ii Jj Kk Ll Mm Nn Oo Pp Qq Rr Ss Tt Uu Vv Ww Xx **Yy** Zz

Zz

Zebra Finch

Zebra finches are one of the most common birds kept as pets. They can lay eggs two months after they themselves hatch. Zebra finches know how to fly when they are born and leave the nest three weeks later.

Note to Teachers and Parents

This book uses the alphabet to introduce children to the world of birds. It is designed to be read aloud to a pre-reader or read independently by an early reader. It shows children that learning through nonfiction books can be fun. Photographs help early readers and listeners understand the text. The book encourages further learning by including a fact-filled glossary, an activity page, and a list of additional books to read and internet sites to visit. Older readers will find the glossary useful in preparing reports and fact-filled compendiums.

Hands-On Projects

Flight Speeds

Activity: Not all birds fly in the same manner. The albatross can soar for hours without flapping its wings, but hummingbirds flap their wings over 70 times a second! Invite children to test their "wings" to see how many times they can flap them in 10 seconds. Have them extend their arms away from their bodies and flap them up and down. Time the number of flaps that can be accomplished in ten seconds.

Facts: A robin has 23 wing beats/10 seconds

A pigeon has 30 wing beats/10 seconds

A chickadee has 270 wing beats/10 seconds

A hummingbird has 700 wing beats/10 seconds

Make a Bird Mosaic

Make an eggshell mosaic of your favorite bird.

Materials: dyed or colored eggshells, construction paper, pencil or pen, glue stick

Directions:
1. Break the shells into small pieces.
2. Trace or draw an outline of your favorite bird.
3. Fill in the outline with glue.
4. Place the eggshell pieces in the glue, forming a colorful mosaic of your bird.
5. Set the mosaic aside to dry.

Challenge children to dictate or write a short story about the bird that they create. Hang children's mosaics for everyone to see and enjoy.

Internet Sites

The Albatross Site
http://www.wfu.edu/albatross/index.htm

The Audubon Kids' Site
http://www.audubon.org/bird/watch/kids/

Birding For Kids
http://birding.tqn.com/msubkids.htm

Curious Facts About Birds
http://www.petersononline.com/birds/bwd/press/1096-answers.html

The Eagle Kids' Home Page
http://www.eaglekids.com

Books About Birds

Boring, Mel. *Birds, Nests, and Eggs. Take-Along Guide.* Minocqua, WI: NorthWord Press, 1996.

Delafosse, Claude. *Birds: A First Discovery Book.* New York: Scholastic, 1993.

Ganeri, Anita. *Birds.* New York: Gloucester Press, 1993.

Johnson, Jinny. *Children's Guide to Birds.* New York: Simon & Schuster, 1996.

Markle, Anita. *Outside and Inside Birds.* New York: Atheneum Books for Young Readers, 1994.

Taylor, Barbara. *The Bird Atlas.* New York: Dorling-Kindersley, 1993.

Glossary

Albatross (Wandering Albatross)
- Member of the albatross family
- Adults grow to 28–53 inches (71–137cm) long
- 13 species worldwide; seven species are found off the coasts of North America

Bobolink
- Member of the *Icteridae* family, which includes blackbirds, orioles, and meadowlarks
- Adults grow to 6–8 inches (15–20cm) long
- Breed in southern Canada and the northern United States; winter in South America

Chickadee (Black-capped Chickadee)
- Member of the titmouse family
- Adults grow to 4–6 inches (10–15cm) long; weigh $\frac{1}{3}$ ounce (9g)
- Found in North American woodlands

Dove (White Dove)
- Member of the pigeon family
- Adults grow to 6–12 inches (15–30cm) long; weigh up to 9 ounces (252g)
- Found in temperate and tropical regions of the world

Eagle (Bald Eagle)
- Member of the hawk family; about 60 species known as eagles or hawks
- Adults grow to 15 pounds (7.2kg) and have a wingspan of 8 feet (240cm)

- Most are found in Africa and Asia; only bald eagles and golden eagles are native to North America

Flamingo (Chilean Flamingo)

- Member of the flamingo family
- Adults grow to 3–5 feet (91–150cm) tall
- Found in Africa, Eurasia, India, West Indies, South America, and Florida

Goldfinch (American Goldfinch)

- Member of the finch family
- Adults grow to 5 inches (13cm) long; weigh ⅓–½ ounce (9–14g)
- The goldfinch is found from southern Canada to Mexico; finches are found in most parts of the world

Hummingbird (Ruby-throated Hummingbird)

- Member of the hummingbird family; includes more than 300 members
- The largest adults grow to about 8 inches (20cm) long; most are about 3 inches (5cm)
- Hummingbirds are found only in the Western Hemisphere

Ibis (Scarlet Ibis)

- Member of the ibis family; includes 20 species of long-legged, long-necked wading birds
- Adults grow to 22–27 inches (55–68cm) long
- Found in warm places around the world

Jay (Blue Jay)

- Member of the crow family, which includes ravens and magpies

- Adults grow to 1 foot (30cm) long
- Found east of the Rocky Mountains in North America

Killdeer

- Member of the plover family; includes 63 species worldwide
- Adults grow to 10 inches (25cm) long
- Found from southern Canada to South America

Loon (Common Loon)

- Member of the loon family; includes four species
- Adults grow to 30 inches (76cm) long
- All loons are found in the Northern Hemisphere

Mockingbird (Northern Mockingbird)

- Member of the mockingbird family; includes 31 species
- Adults grow to 9–11 inches (23–28cm) long
- Found from the northern United States to Mexico and in the West Indies

Nightingale

- Member of the thrush family
- Adults grow to 6 inches (15cm) long
- Found throughout Europe

Ostrich

- Member of the ostrich family
- Adults grow to 9 feet (2.4m) tall and weigh up to 330 pounds (150kg)
- Live on the plains and deserts of Africa

Puffin (Horned Puffin)

- Member of the auk family; includes three species
- Adults grow to 13 inches (34cm) long, wingspan of 21–24 inches (53–61cm)
- Found in the Arctic waters of the North Atlantic (Iceland, Greenland, Canada, United States) and Pacific (Alaska) Oceans

Quail (California Quail)

- Member of the pheasant family; includes 45 species
- Adults grow 8–12 inches (20–30cm) long
- Found in almost every part of the world

Roadrunner (Greater Roadrunner)

- Member of the cuckoo family
- Adults grow to 2 feet (61cm) long
- Found in the deserts of the southwestern United States and Mexico

Swan (Mute Swan)

- Member of the *Anatidae* family; includes geese and ducks
- The largest adult swans grow to 4 feet (122cm) tall and weigh 21–30 lbs (12–14kg)
- Live in Europe, Australia, Asia, and North and South America

Turkey (Wild Turkey)

- Member of wild turkey family; includes two species; there are several species of domestic turkeys
- The largest adults grow to 36–48 inches (91–122cm) long; weigh 23–35 pounds (12-14kg)
- Found in the eastern and southern United States to Mexico and Guatemala

Upland Sandpiper

- Member of the sandpiper family
- Adults grow to 11–12 inches (28–31cm) long
- Breed in North America; winter in South America

Vulture (Lappet-faced Vulture)

- Member of the New World vulture family; includes 7 species
- Adults grow 22–27 inches (56–69cm) long, wingspan of 54–60 inches (137–152cm)
- Found in North and South America

Woodpecker (Pileated Woodpecker)

- Member of the woodpecker family; includes 210 species
- Adults grow to 3–23 inches (8–58cm) long
- Found in most woodland areas except Australia and New Guinea

Xanthocephalus xanthocephalus (Yellow-headed Blackbird)

- Member of the blackbird family
- Adults grow to 8 inches (21cm) long
- Found in North America

Yellow-billed Oxpecker

- Member of the *Sturnidae* family
- Adults grow to 9 inches (23cm) long
- Found in tropical Africa outside evergreen forests

Zebra Finch

- Member of the finch family
- Adults grow to 3–4 inches (8–10cm) long
- The zebra finch is found only in Australia; finches are found in most parts of the world

Index

A+ Books are published by Capstone Press
P.O. Box 669, Mankato, Minnesota 56002
http://www.capstone-press.com

EDITORIAL CREDITS:

Susan Evento, Managing Editor/Product Development; Don L. Curry, Senior Editor; Jannike Hess, Designer; Kimberly Danger and Heidi Schoof, Photo Researchers; Content Consultant: Ilze Balodis

LIBRARY OF CONGRESS CATALOGING-IN-PUBLICATION DATA:

DeGezelle, Terri, 1955-
     Birds A to Z/by Terri DeGezelle
          p.   cm.
     Includes bibliographical references.
     Summary: Introduces the world of birds through photographs and facts which describe one for each letter of the alphabet.
     ISBN 0-7368-7038-5 (hard) — ISBN 0-7368-7049-0 (paper)
     1. Birds–Juvenile literature. 2. English language–Alphabet–Juvenile literature. [1. Birds. 2. Alphabet.] I. Title.
     QL676.2 .D396 2000
     598–dc21   99-052403

PHOTO CREDITS:

Cover: Arthur Morris/Visuals Unlimited; *Title Page:* Cheryl Ertelt; *Page 2:* Tom Brakefield/Bruce Coleman Inc.; *Page 3:* Robert McCaw; *Page 4:* Barbara Gerlach/Visuals Unlimited; *Page 5:* Taurus Photos/Photophile; *Page 6:* Robert E. Barber; *Page 7:* Robert E. Barber; *Page 8:* Dwight Kuhn; *Page 9:* Anthony Mercicca/Photophile; *Page 10:* Joe McDonald/Visuals Unlimited; *Page 11:* Robert McCaw; *Page 12:* Robert McCaw; *Page 13:* Robert McCaw; *Page 14:* Richard Day/Daybreak Imagery; *Page 15:* Hans Reinhard/Bruce Coleman Inc.; *Page 16:* Tom & Pat Leeson; *Page 17:* Robert E. Barber; *Page 18:* Photri; *Page 19:* Joe McDonald/Visuals Unlimited; *Page 20:* Barrett & MacKay Photo; *Page 21:* Lee Kline; *Page 22:* John Gerlach/Visuals Unlimited; *Page 23:* Gerald Tang; *Page 24:* Byron Jorjorian; *Page 25:* Joe McDonald; *Page 26:* Joe McDonald; *Page 27:* Rob and Ann D. Simpson